DEAR PARENTS,

NOTES FROM
A CHILD
OF DIVORCE

Grace Casper

Dear Parents: Notes From a Child of Divorce

© 2023 by Grace Casper

Published in Waco, TX by Divorce Tips From Kids

ISBN 979-8-9883595-0-0 (ebook)
ISBN 979-8-9883595-1-7 (paperback)
ISBN 979-8-9883595-2-4 (audiobook)

Cover Design: ebooklaunch
Author Photo: H.D. Tolson

To Mom and Dad.

Without you, none of this would have been possible.
Thank you for making the right decision for yourselves and our
family. Thank you for letting me speak out on the effects of
divorce on children without wondering if you both approve.
You've taught me that we are not broken, but whole.

Love,

Grace ♡

CONTENTS

Introduction

Acknowledgments

INTRODUCTION

When I look at the expansive collection of resources
for those going through divorce, I see there are many great
options. However, there is one major gap, which is the lack
of resources from the kid's perspective—kids of divorce,
specifically. Sure, there are authors who are children of
divorce, but their writing is from their own post-divorce,
adult voice. Those voices are needed and bring a lot to the
table, but what I wanted to see was a book written by a kid
for families going through divorce. There are a few
options out there but, as far as I know, they were published
over 20 years ago and don't contain any practical advice,
just perspective sharing. I didn't know it at the time, but I
would soon come to desire to be the one to fill this gap. To
preserve my younger voice, allow her to introduce
herself...

2010:

Hi, I am Gracie Bug! Well, that's what my dad calls me. You aren't allowed to call me that. I am a big girl. I mean, I *am* a fifth grader! So I prefer Grace. I go to school at Buffalo Ridge Elementary in Castle Pines, Colorado. But I don't live there anymore. After my parents divorced, my mom moved my brother and me to Parker, Colorado. I told her I could *not* move to a new school again, so we drive 40 minutes everyday so I can finish up elementary school at Buffalo Ridge. This year I started something scary: it's called "counseling." Basically, I have to talk to this adult about my worries and my parent's divorce. I don't really get what it does. I do know that afterwards though, I feel really light—almost like a feather! My counselor told me I should try journaling, so I started writing notes for my brother and me from going house to house with divorced parents.

NOW:

What I present you with today, is a book based on the notes I originally wrote on the playground during recess in the fifth grade. I decided to write to you, parents, because you set the tone of the home. You are the models for your kids. Kids need hope in this time, and they need adults that are ready to step up to the plate for them. Your kids *need* you!

Before you start diving into each note, I want you to get to know me and my story more. I recognize that every divorce story is different, and this is just mine. However, I believe the things I learned from my parents' divorce are not just for me to share with my counselor and younger brother, but are also for you, the parent seeking help on how to navigate divorce as you, initially, explain this separation to your child and, continuously, begin to live and experience this separation.

My parents got divorced, after being married for twelve years, when I was in the third grade. I still remember the day that my mom sat my younger brother and me down on the family room couch.

"Dad and I are getting a divorce."

I knew I was supposed to act sad, but I didn't know why because, ultimately, I didn't *understand* divorce and all that it entailed. I didn't realize that divorce meant their marriage was ending, that Jack and I would have to grow up traveling between houses, that we would have two of every holiday, and that coordinating schedules and communication would be very hard. I started counseling in the fifth grade, and my counselor told me I should write out my feelings.

My first draft was born from this, in the pages of my composition notebook at recess. I wrote down 10 bullet points, or "tips," for going between houses to give to my little brother, Jack. When I brought this home, my mom said I needed to show my counselor, Sharon. Sharon was amazed by the writing and told me that it could very well be a book one day, but I didn't believe her.

How could a kid be an author?

She told me that she could give it to her agent and he could show it to a few publishers and see what they think. This led to countless rejections. I was told I was too young, that the genre and audience of the book was too confusing, and there were far too many logistic obstacles to overcome in its creation.

Fast forward to college, and I still couldn't get that book off my mind. I wasn't even an English major, as I was studying business at Baylor University. After meeting with mentors and going to an event called "Dream Big Framework," I realized I needed to finish what I started at age 10. However, I needed to change it to be a book for parents, as they were the ones I really wanted to talk to. Through a lot of restructuring, writer's block, and late nights, I finally finished writing. I believe this was hard to write not because of word count but because of the context—it was hard to think back on my lived experience of my parents' divorce while growing up. But, ultimately, it was healing for me to put such experiences into words for others to relate to and be comforted by. With that, I hope you see the rare treasure in this work. You are holding something that was championed for over 10 years of my life.

My desire is for this book to be a catalyst for conversation, and that you can learn what your children might need from you in your divorce—because they *do* need you. They need you now more than ever, because their lives are changing just as much as yours. I hope my perspective from being one of those children can offer you some starting points on how to do this with confidence, love, and success.

Do you feel ready for this? I believe in you.

1

FINDING A SCHEDULE FOR YOUR KIDS

• • •

Scheduling is one of the hardest logistical problems post-divorce. It's tough to say goodbye to your kids when they go to the other parent's house. I know it's not only me that feels this way. Back in January, I took an Instagram poll of my followers, who tend to be a mixture of both parents and kids, and the majority voted that transition days were described as "stressful." It will take a bit of time until you land on what works for your family. Let me give you some backstory as to how my family landed on our schedule.

My dad is one of the hardest workers I know. He was still in college when my older half-sister was born, and it didn't even interrupt his schooling. After graduating, he worked for an insurance company and traveled quite often while I was growing up—so I was used to Dad being gone on business trips.

When the divorce happened, I thought I was going to be splitting time with my mom and my dad so it would be equal—I loved when things were fair. In court, however, joint custody was not the final decision. This is an aspect that kids, *especially* young kids, have no part in deciding.

Now that I am older and know more of my family's story, I understand it. I understand that as a parent you have one million things going on in your head. You begin to comprehend and mourn the loss of your marriage and yet you are also trying to stay strong for your children and make smart decisions. As a kid, I didn't even know that court or mediation was going on in the background. One of the reasons why was because my mom was good at shielding us from it all by taking us to her friend's house for "playdates" with her kids. Meanwhile, I just thought that going to Ms. Heidi's house for several hours, multiple times a week was normal! Little did I know the conversations that were being had on my behalf behind the scenes.

As the parent, you have the luxury of controlling the process and making the calls. While I know that every situation is unique, and you may feel like your co-parent called all of the shots, remember that it is still *a* parent calling the shots—*never* the child.

At the very least, I want you to consider putting your own needs to the side and asking your children how they feel about moving from house to house. Do not take their answer personally; if they like being at Dad's house more, it may not be because of Dad. Many children are very routine-oriented, so it might be the atmosphere of the home, or its closer proximity to school or their friends.

I lived and grew up in the same neighborhood until the divorce. It was a classic, sheltered, suburban neighborhood. When my dad moved into an all-glass apartment in Denver, it was a big change.

I am not saying that change is bad, but rather that kids thrive off structure, familiarity, and routine.

So, going to the glass tower felt completely out of my comfort zone of suburbia. It was cool to look out and see the city, but it was also very overwhelming to constantly hear sirens, honking, and street fights. My dad moved out to the glass tower so my mom could keep the family home we were in. With all that was available to him, a one-bedroom apartment was the pick. Which meant a blanket fort for my brother and I. I remember gathering up all of the blankets and pillows to built a nest on the hardwood floors. It was nestled within this cocoon that I fell in love with Hallmark's *25 Days of Christmas* and found out that the Tooth Fairy was actually my dad. Isn't it funny what kids remember?

Due to the drastic difference between Mom's house that I grew up in and Dad's glass tower, I needed more time at the former. Through trial and error, we discovered I needed two weekends in a row with my mom to be ready for a change of scenery at my dad's. Again, this didn't mean Dad's place was worse because, frankly, it wasn't. It was simply a lot of change for a 10-year-old to go through, and two weekends at Mom's gave me more time to hang out with my friends. Of course, there were times when friends' birthday parties would fall on one of the weekends with Dad. In those scenarios I would let my dad know and either come after the party or just go to his house the next weekend!

You can see from just this short explanation how changes that come with divorce for a young child can be disorienting. As best as you can, you will want to retain a schedule or rhythm that your child can quickly adopt. This isn't only for their benefit, but also for yours. A schedule allows you to know how much time to expect with your kids. Without this, it can feel like constant whiplash and, let me tell you, that's no fun for *anyone* involved.

LET'S GET PRACTICAL...

Sometimes the best thing is to sit your kids down and ask them what their thoughts are on the schedule. You can make this a one-time thing, or you can check in often—weekly or monthly—to make sure it's still working for everyone.

One of my podcast guests, Sara Olsher (divorced, coparent, and mom of one), creates her daughter's schedule with her weekly. Sara always makes sure that they plan something fun for the night her daughter comes back to her house. This makes transition days something to look forward to and hopefully less stressful.

ACTION PLAN

Find what kind of calendar works for you! There are visual magnetic calendars (see other resource list below), paper calendars, online calendars, and more!

FOR YOUR CONSIDERATION/GOING DEEPER

1.) When you think about your own childhood, what times did you feel like life was unpredictable? Did you have a routine as a kid? Did this help at all?

_____

_____

_____

_____

_____

_____

_____

_____

2.) How can you improve communication with your co-parent around your children's scheduling needs? Where can you work on being more flexible for your kids?

_____

_____

_____

_____

_____

_____

_____

_____

_____

_____

3.) How can you make transition day a better experience for your kids?

_____

_____

_____

_____

_____

_____

_____

_____

_____

_____

_____

Further Reading / Other Resources*:

- *Home Sweet Homes Journal* by Fiona Kong — A journal with prompts and a calendar with weeks and months. Options for child, mom, and dad to all participate in.

- Mighty and Bright Magnetic Visual Calendars — A week-long calendar. A visual way for your kids to keep track of when they spend time with mom or dad and other fun things. This provides empowerment and ownership of their own lives.

- Family Core App — An app with an online calendar feature, secure document storage, group chats, and location tracking.

*all of the resources listed throughout the book can be found on my website at:

divorcetipsfromkids.com/other-resources

Scan with your phone

2

DON'T FORGET THAT KIDS NEED FUN

• • •

Going through a divorce is a somber affair for every member of the family, and in particular for the kids. They may feel like they will never ever again experience fun or see Mom and Dad have fun, which can be a devastating thought to a child, especially younger ones. For a teen, fun can mean a myriad of different things, but fun could also make them feel like you are ignoring the sadness of divorce. This could add to the heaviness of the separation.

It will be important to consider the role of fun in your family's newfound circumstances and the age of your kids.

You might be the parent who lives further away from your kids' friends, and that can make it harder for the kids to have fun since they aren't having play dates as frequently. But, have no fear, you are creative whether you think so or not. How? You have a wonderful tool either in your hand or in your pocket: a smart phone. Lucky for you, you don't have to come up with grand, extravagant ideas for you and your kids to enjoy—the Pinterest moms have done it for you.

The ideas you will find on that platform are full of fun. You can search "crafts for kids," "activities for teens," or even "sensory activities." However, I want to encourage you to go there *after* you've brainstormed ideas on your own. Ultimately, you know your kids best, better than the Super Mom on Pinterest.

I remember I was so excited to go to my dad's house after he'd tell my brother and me that he had fun activities planned for us. Since he lived downtown, these activities included bowling, watching a movie, or going to our favorite restaurant and playing hangman on the paper menus. Ultimately, your child wants to know that you are excited to spend time with them.

If you are on a tight budget because of, well, *divorce*, you can still plan activities. As I mentioned in the previous chapter, my brother and I loved building forts. Forts are totally free. At my mom's house, we would do "smorgasbord nights." This was when we would examine the pantry, freezer, and fridge to see what we could create and share with one another.

My mom would usually make thin, German pancakes with warm maple syrup, I would make a toasted PB&J with cheddar cheese on the side, and my brother would eat beef jerky and Oreos. It was amazing. It was even more fun when we could queue our favorite songs throughout the night and have them play in the background. The vibe would start with Michael Bublé, switch to Hannah Montana, then end with Crazy Frog. We had quite the mix.

If your kids are older, this is a great opportunity to empower them to come up with their own ideas. Allow them to take the lead by putting them in charge of planning a fun evening for the next time they are with you. This gives them something to look forward to.

Keep in mind that after planning such an evening, they want one thing from you: affirmation. Whether the evening is a flop or a total success, your child wants you to recognize their hard work in planning a night. Tell them it was fun, worth it, and that they are creative.

The study of "fun" is quite interesting. I know that I always needed to be reminded that my parents were with me not just for my accolades and achievements, but because they enjoyed spending time with me. Research done by Dr. Michael Popkin, Psychiatrist and founder of Active Parenting Publishers, states that "playing with your child builds the child's self-esteem, helps the child learn about the world, provides opportunities for the child to learn new skills, and builds the bond between parent and child."[1]

I know you might get annoyed with your child saying "Mom/Dad watch this!" or "Can you play with me?" but these invitations are not going to be around forever. These are tiny moments where your child sends a signal in hopes of connecting with you. These tiny moments add up over time and make an impact. Will you accept the invitation?

LET'S GET PRACTICAL...

You may have one week when you are exhausted and don't have the energy to plan. That's okay, you're human

---

[1] Popkin, M. H. (2017). Chapter 1: Every Day a Little Play. In *Active Parenting First Five Years* (pp. 33–37). Active Parenting Publishers.

after all. But instead of scrambling when they arrive, you can prepare for these moments by investing in one thing: backpacks. Let your child pack their "fun backpacks" with their favorite toys, coloring books, movies, puzzles, and snacks. Do you see what I did there? I didn't say, "Pack their backpacks with a tablet."

I am not saying tablets are bad for kids, but I believe they can still have fun without electronic devices—my brother and I did it! We didn't have phones or touch screen anything until the eighth grade! I know times are changing, but I really do believe your kid can still race origami boats outside, play make believe chef, and fight with action figures. And if you're on a budget, give your kids a set amount of money and let them pick out whatever they want to play with at the dollar store. This way anytime you hit a wall, you can just tell your kids to go play with their fun backpacks for 30 minutes.

ACTION PLAN

Buy one of your favorite nostalgic toys you liked having when growing up. It can be used as a reminder to plan fun things with your kids even without the use of tablets.

FOR YOUR CONSIDERATION/GOING DEEPER

1.) When was the last time you had fun with your kids? What did it feel like to do something "unproductive" and carefree with them?

_____

_____

_____

_____

_____

_____

_____

_____

2.) Write down three people or places where you could get inspiration from to help you brainstorm ideas for you and your kids.

_____

_____

_____

_____

_____

_____

_____

_____

3.) Why do you think it is valuable for your kids to learn that they can just have fun with you without any other expectations?

_____

_____

_____

_____

_____

_____

_____

_____

_____

Further Reading / Other Resources:

- *The Power of Fun* by Catherine Price — a book on how fun can empower your kids and increase bonding between you and your child.

3

MODEL HOW TO DEAL WITH WORRIES

• • •

In my family, I have always been the anxious one. I don't know if it's just my nature or if it is a result of what I've been through. Either way, I have high-functioning anxiety. If you had asked me what anxiety was when I was in the fourth grade, I would have no idea what to make of the word. It wasn't until the fifth grade, when I started seeing a counselor, where I learned the word "anxiety."

It was nice having a word to describe my jumbled worries and random "what ifs." Counseling changed my life—it's a huge part of my *life* story, not just my divorce story. It was so refreshing to talk to someone who was totally removed from my situation and wouldn't just comfort me but said things as they were with no sugar coating.

I learned many things about myself through counseling, but the best was the practical tips on how to manage my anxiety. I understand that not every child deals with anxiety, but that doesn't mean they don't get worried from time to time. So, if you think counseling is too expensive, or your child doesn't need it, I would still like to share with you one of the biggest superpowers I've ever encountered: journaling.

Journaling for some is an activity only relegated to time spent with a counselor or therapist. I'd encourage you to rethink that and consider a journal as a wonderful tool for yourself as well as your kids.

Journals come in all sizes and formats; you can even find some journals that have blank pages on one side and lines on the other or, for the younger kids, ones that are split in half with the top half of the page blank to draw and the bottom half with lines. The options are endless. Journaling is such a superpower because it's the one place where there are no rules. You can write big, you can write small, you can even *cuss*. You can use a pencil or marker, you can draw. Journaling is such a good outlet to let any thought hit the paper, no matter how weird, scary, or embarrassing it might be.

I am a big believer in making everyday things *big deals*. If you want to encourage your child to write, show them you are in it with them.

Make a big deal out of picking out a journal and a writing tool. This is not your everyday shopping trip; this is a big deal. This is the start of putting all of those bottled-up thoughts into something that can hold them for you.

Your family can take a trip to Target or Barnes & Noble and look at the journals—there are some with lines, some with dots, some with grids, and some blank. Or, if you really want to take this to the next level, you can decorate your own journal. You can get blank, covered journals (my favorite brand is Moleskine) and then use magazine cutouts, crayons, or paint to decorate and make your journals personal. I understand to some this may sound "too girly," but we limit boys when we do not give them art as an outlet. You know your child best, so if they aren't into crafts, then just get them a basic journal.

Before your child goes off with their new tool, explain the rules to them. Here are some suggestions that worked in my home:

1. You can write absolutely anything in your journal.
2. No one is allowed to read your journal without your permission.
3. There are no rules on how to write or what to write in your journal.

Now, I can hear the over-protective parent saying something along the lines of, "But I need to read my child's journal in order to know what's actually going on with them." And yes, wanting to know your kids' feelings is an honorable and good thing to want to know, but it's not the right way to do it.

Instead, it should be your priority to make sure your kids feel validated which will help them feel more comfortable talking with you, sharing how they feel and asking questions. Reading a child's journal without their permission will cause a breaking of trust, and that's hard to rebuild.

LET'S GET PRACTICAL...

If you didn't grow up in a home where it was normal to share your emotions, you're probably not sure how to make that space in your own home. That's okay. Get committed to finding a way to get better. Consider reading a book, talking with a close friend, working with a counselor or looking for someone you admire who seems skilled in this area.

You cannot teach your kids how to express their emotions if you can't do it yourself. This goes with so many other, simpler things—you can't teach your kids how to do laundry if you don't know how to do it. Working on yourself will give you a space to express how you feel and help you build practical skills that you can use at home with your kids.

My mom did a wonderful job at this. Whenever we would talk "real-talk" (meaning the divorce, bullying at school, or any other hard topics), we could say anything we wanted to. We could cuss, we could yell, we could cry. She made space for us to lay it all on the table so that we wouldn't shove it all down or blow up on someone at school.

My brother and I didn't know how to do this naturally, so my mom would have us eat dinners together at the table, which is where most of these conversations happened. It took her asking good questions and listening to our answers that made us feel safe. My mom wouldn't judge what we said, correct us, or lecture us. She simply listened, acknowledged and validated what we were saying, and ended it all with a big hug. Most of the time we don't need a solution to our problems or worries, we just need to be heard—so don't stress about having the right words, but instead focus on having a genuine interest in what your kids are going through.

ACTION PLAN

Figure out what you need to do to get better at dealing with *your* worries, before trying to help your child deal with theirs.

FOR YOUR CONSIDERATION/GOING DEEPER

1.) What keeps you from addressing your scary thoughts or worries?

_____

_____

_____

_____

_____

_____

_____

_____

2.) What kind of journaling do you want to adopt? Daily update entries? Journal prompts? Gratitude lists? Voice memo journaling? What works best for you?

_____

_____

_____

_____

_____

_____

_____

_____

3.) How can you lead your child through their anxious thoughts? What ways can you show them their feelings are valid and that they are safe with you?

_____

_____

_____

_____

_____

_____

4

SEND A PIECE OF YOURSELF WITH YOUR KIDS

• • •

We all know the five senses: touch, smell, sight, sound, and taste. All five are a gift that allow us to experience all that life has to offer. But did you know that smell has the most "elevated status" among the five? Some think it may be due to our ancestors having to use their sense of smell to find food. The science behind it all is *wild* to me. In a Harvard Gazette article, it's noted that, "Smells are handled by the olfactory bulb, the structure in the front of the brain that sends information to the other areas of the body's central command for further processing. Odors take a direct route to the limbic system, including the amygdala and the hippocampus, the regions related to emotion and memory."[2] This explains why a smell can trigger a certain memory or emotion with such clarity and intensity.

I am sure your kids know your smell. Maybe they recall that Dad smells of cologne or cigarette smoke, or maybe Mom smells of essential oils or a certain body wash. Do you remember the scent you picked up as a child from your parents?

For me, the scent of my mom was unique to her; it was a mix of her laundry detergent, face lotion, and deodorant, and it was wonderful. All her shirts had her specific scent. Sometimes, I would miss my mom when I was at my dad's house, just wanting a big hug from her.

When I explained this to her, she gave me one of her T-shirts. The next time I went over to my dad's house, I brought this piece of my mom with me and it felt like she

---

[2] Hammer, Ashley. "Here's Why Smells Trigger Such Vivid Memories." *Discovery*, 1 Aug. 2019, www.discovery.com/science/Why-Smells-Trigger-Such-Vivid-Memories.

was right next to me when I smelled it. I did the same with my dad. His smell was a mix of his cologne and a specific minty gum, and I chose to take his big comfy Air Force Academy sweatshirt with me to my mom's. I have the best memories of going with him to the Air Force Academy football games and watching the flyovers before the start of every game. Smelling big shirts may sound a little odd but, in my family, hugs and physical affection is how we show love. When I would smell that shirt, it felt like a big 'ole hug from my parent who wasn't with me at the time.

Your family might be different, but your kids will probably still miss you when they are at the other parent's house, even if you aren't big huggers. So, figure out what part of you can be made into travel-sized comfort. Kids don't like packing things back and forth from house to house. If we can have pieces of consistency it makes things easier. So if you have a kid that's struggling with missing you at the other parent's house, sending something may be a good idea. This could be your scent through a T-shirt, your jokes written out, a bracelet you make with them, or an audio clip of your voice reading their favorite book to them.

LET'S GET PRACTICAL...

Normally at this point I would break this down to something practical and applicable to daily life. This chapter in and of itself is already practical. The only thing I will add is try not to take offense if your child needs a piece of the other parent at your house; this says nothing about you or how they feel towards you.

Remember, they have *two* parents whom they can love and miss simultaneously. Additionally, this comfort doesn't have an expiration date—if your child is a teenager and still carries around a blanket or item of clothing from you, let them. When they are ready to grow up and move on, they will, but if this can help them make the pain of the divorce a little less hurtful for now, it's worth it.

ACTION PLAN

Sit down as a family and talk about what makes up your signature scent. You might be surprised and get a kick out of what smells your children know you by.

FOR YOUR CONSIDERATION/GOING DEEPER

1.) What scents remind you of a good or comforting memory? What scents bring you back to a bad one?

_____

_____

_____

_____

_____

_____

_____

_____

2.) Think of the five senses. How might you be able to use one or more of the five senses to offer your child comfort when they miss you or the other parent?

_____

_____

_____

_____

_____

_____

_____

_____

3.) What things will you put in place with your co-parent to make sure your child feels safe bringing a comfort item to the different houses?

_____

_____

_____

_____

_____

_____

_____

_____

Further Reading / Other Resources:

- *Life in Five Senses* by Gretchen Rubin—A powerful book on how exploring her five senses got her out of her head and into the world.

5

ALLOW YOUR KIDS TO LOVE IN THEIR WAY

• • •

As I touched on in the previous chapter, sometimes kids will want to do something with one parent and not the other. Yes, just like parents sometimes have favorites, kids do too. Don't be discouraged as these are usually seasonal. At different times in my life, and at different ages, I needed both parents in new ways. When I was younger, my mom was my go-to. I was always hugging her, calling her, wanting her for everything. I'm sure that wasn't easy for my dad to watch.

However, that changed when hormones hit, and I became annoyed with everything—including mom. All the sudden I wanted to have dinners with my dad more. I preferred going to his house and I started to appreciate the city life. I can't quite explain why, but he was easier to spend time with. I know my mom was a bit hurt by that. Looking back though, they each got their own season of me favoring one more than the other.

Every kid is different, and I know my brother has had his fair share of times leaning on one parent more than the other. It may not look like the picture that I painted of my experience. But I wanted to talk about it to make you aware.

When your child is leaning on the other parent more than you, don't take it as a personal attack. It's more than likely that you are not doing anything wrong. So, no need to beat yourself up for it. Remember that your kid will need you and your co-parent in different ways at different times. If they are leaning more on the other parent right now, I promise they will need you again.

What would push them further away from you is guilting them for what they are doing with your co-parent. Letting jealousy get the best of you will not be worth it. In hosting my podcast, *Divorce: What I Wish My Parents Knew*, I have heard countless stories from children of divorce explaining the guilt they felt from parents. They wanted to balance their love and attention because showing any signs of favoritism would create anger and bitterness in the other parent.

Please don't blame your child for their favoritism. It's natural to need mom or dad in one season more than another. Going above and beyond for your child would be affirming the time they are spending with your co-parent. Saying something like, "I'm glad you have your dad to do those things with" would create such safety and a moment of relief for your child. They can let go of the fear of hurting your feelings when telling you how fun it was.

Now, they have the verbal affirmation that you are mature enough to recognize there are some things that your co-parent can do that you cannot do. I know many kids who were starving for this kind of affirmation from one or both of their parents. They never wanted to hurt their mom or dad in having fun at the other parent's house.

LET'S GET PRACTICAL...

You may have picked up by now that I am a huge fan of writing things out. For this exercise, make the chart with the categories as I have listed below. This exercise lets you view things centered on the benefits of the kids. You can write out the things that may make you upset or jealous but recognize that you too can offer things to your kids. It's not a competition—all you can do is show up for your kids in the ways that you know how and remind them that they are deeply loved and safe with you.

Things my co-parent does	How it serves our kids	Things I can do for our kids
1. Taking them to fancy dinners that I can't afford. 2. My co-parent loves the outdoors and takes the kids camping.	1. The kids get to experience new things and try foods that can expand their palate. 2. This teaches them to go outside of their comfort zone and learn about the outdoors.	1. I can make homemade meals that they recognize and feel familiar with. This can bring them a sense of consistency. 2. I can take them to museums and teach them about history and science!

ACTION PLAN

Start writing out your three-column chart. Be proud of what *you* can offer your kid. It is needed and valued, even if your kids don't explicitly say it now.

They will thank you one day.

FOR YOUR CONSIDERATION/GOING DEEPER

1.) When did you favor one of your parents instead of the other growing up? Did you feel guilty for favoring one over another?

_____

_____

_____

_____

_____

_____

_____

2.) How can you reassure your children that they don't need to filter themselves when they talk about their other parent?

_____

_____

_____

_____

_____

_____

_____

3.) What are ways that you can validate or reinforce for your children that you are happy if they are happy?

_____

_____

_____

_____

_____

_____

_____

_____

_____

_____

_____

_____

_____

_____

_____

6

REMIND THEM OF YOUR LOVE

• • •

This is probably one of the most important chapters to me. Divorce sucks. I am not going to lie. It does. And maybe in your family it isn't okay to say that, but let's just admit it is a devastating event for all involved—parents *and* their kids. It gets better! You'll know this after you read my chapter titled, "It's Not Broken, It's Whole."

But besides being devastating, it is *confusing*. For a child who maybe hasn't seen the harder parts of your relationship behind closed doors—which, by the way, is a

35

good thing—it can be confusing trying to figure out why Mom and Dad are wanting to separate.

I saw my parents fight at times. In fact, my brother and I had a little space called The Honeycomb Hideout where we'd escape to if they were fighting; we had a DVD player, Oreos, and stuffed animals. Even though I saw some of their fights, I was still so confused as to why Dad was moving out and why Mom and he were getting a divorce.

I can remember thinking—What even *is* a divorce?

I heard a couple of kids in my class talk about their parents having the same thing, but I didn't know what it was. My mom tried to explain it as best as she could, to a first and third grader, but my brother and I were still lost.

I think the first time it hit me was when we went to Dad's new house, and part of me started to wonder why the divorce happened. I never thought to attribute it to their fighting, but instead immediately blamed myself. Was it because I wouldn't listen to them sometimes? Was it because I hugged Mom more? Was it because I watched football with Dad and not Mom? I was so confused. My parents caught onto this pretty quickly, and I distinctly remember having two separate conversations with each of them.

They both emphasized to me that their divorce had nothing to do with me or my brother. It was something that was totally between them. My dad said, "Sometimes people get divorced, but that doesn't mean I hate your mom. We are still friends."

I know that may sound repulsive to you if you have a lot of bitterness towards your co-parent, but my dad's comment made me feel better.

However, even with their separate conversations with me and my dad's nice comment, I still felt at fault. And that's why I wrote this tip as a fifth grader—I didn't want Jack or myself to doubt that Mom and Dad still loved us just the same after their divorce.

Divorce is already so full of sadness, mourning, and loss, which is why love is needed all the more and to its fullest extent. You may think that you are just annoying your kids in reminding them how much you love them, and to that I say, what a *good* problem to have.

This is an area in which over-communication is key. I am not suggesting to say the phrase, "I love you"—which *is* powerful and needed daily—but I mean showing love through your actions as well. If your child is younger, they may not know what makes them feel loved yet, and that is, in a sense, fun, because you get to try it all.

If you haven't read the book *The Five Love Languages* by Gary Chapman, I recommend it. The five love languages are acts of service, words of affirmation, gifts, quality time, and physical touch.

You have the chance to shower your kid with all of these until they grow older and start to know what specifically makes them feel loved. For me, I would much rather have a meaningful conversation (quality time) or a hug (physical touch) than receive a gift. But *your* child may love receiving gifts or being encouraged through words of affirmation.

If you're thinking to yourself, "Well, I'm not good at encouraging people, I stumble with my words" or "Hugs make me feel weird," I ask you to consider learning how to be uncomfortable and try those things if that is what makes your child feel seen and known.

I have a friend who has never heard her father say he is proud of her. She knows he supports her and loves her, but that little part of her still wonders, "If I've never heard him say it, how do I actually know he really feels that way?" This friend is a full-blown *adult*. Maybe you have even felt this with your parents. Either way, make it your mission to ensure that your kids feel loved and affirmed.

LET'S GET PRACTICAL...

How can you show your kids that you love them with your actions? Plain and simple: show up. There is something so special in attending your kid's events, whether it's a soccer game, school play, or dance recital. You might be thinking, "I have a huge report I need to write up for my boss and my daughter will only be on stage for five minutes of this five-hour recital."

Show up.

Christina McGhee—divorce coach, author, and founder of *Divorce and Children*—says, "What matters most to kids is not the presents you buy them but the presence you play in their lives."

Know the dates for these things as early as possible so you can work around them. The feeling of being on stage or on the field and looking around for your parents is like searching for a lifeboat when lost at sea. When you finally see that they are there, you feel safe, supported, and loved. There's also the excitement of pointing them out to teammates or dance partners. Kids are always asking, "Which one is your parent?" Having to respond that one's parents couldn't make it is the worst.

Please hear me when I say that you don't have to be perfect with this. You are only human, as I have repeatedly said. I understand that you may have multiple kids with multiple events, or maybe your relationship with your co-parent is high conflict.

If you have a high conflict co-parent, then bring a friend with you for support and sit on the other side of the arena or field. If that can't happen, then resort to taking turns going to the events. Remember that you are doing this for your kid. You are showing them that you are in their corner. You want to be their biggest fan.

ACTION PLAN

Think about how you can make events more comfortable for your child. Think ahead of time about how you will handle your feelings about seeing the other parent.

FOR YOUR CONSIDERATION/GOING DEEPER

1.) What are your love languages? Do you think you know what kind of affection your kid likes to receive?

_____

_____

_____

_____

_____

_____

_____

_____

_____

_____

_____

_____

2.) How can you reassure your children that your divorce is not their fault?

_____

_____

_____

_____

_____

_____

_____

_____

_____

_____

_____

_____

_____

3.) What are some ways you can reinforce to your children that they are loved? Is it showing up to events? Is it packing them a lunch? Is it asking them about their favorite book or video game?

_____

_____

_____

_____

_____

_____

_____

_____

_____

_____

_____

_____

_____

_____

_____

_____

7

THE POWER OF PETS

• • •

Growing up, I always wanted a dog. In fact, I asked for a stuffed dog for my birthday one year and "potty-trained" it by bringing it outside twice a day. This was all in the effort to convince my parents that I could handle the responsibility of a dog.

Despite my best efforts, they were not convinced.

I always loved going over to my friend's houses and cuddling with their dogs, especially the little ones. One of the main reasons our family didn't get a dog was because my dad was never too keen on having animals around—

which is totally fair, to each their own. By the time I was in the second grade, I finally accepted the reality that my family would probably never get a dog.

However, six months after the divorce, my wish came true. My mom, little brother, and I were in our little apartment and my mom told us the big news: we were going to look at puppies ... but probably weren't going to get one. Jack and I were both ecstatic to see the puppies and sad that we weren't going to get one just yet.

Fuzzy Pups, the breeder's home, was 40 minutes away from our apartment and, as we got closer and closer, I could feel the excitement rushing through my veins. When we pulled up, we heard little barks and saw white, brown, grey, and black puff balls running around outside. The owner came up to us and welcomed us into her home, giving us a tour and showing us all the little pups.

We were coming to the tail end of our tour when we saw *him*; he was sleeping with his fluffy head between his two small paws while other puppies were jumping all around him.

All three of us noticed him at the same time, and Jack said, "What about that one? Can we see him?"

The lady picked up the sleepy boy and let him come meet us. He immediately started wagging his tail and welcomed us with puppy kisses. I looked over at my mom and she was staring at the dog with awe and wonder, telling the breeder that we'd take him home, at which Jack and I looked at her with disbelief. We couldn't believe she saw what we saw in this dog—that he was meant to be ours.

On the car ride home, we decided to name him Sammy Theodore Casper. While Jack and I were cuddling with him in the back of the car, my mom was crying on the phone with her sister. She said, "Shell, it's a miracle. I don't know what it is, but something about this dog is healing."

My mom was right, as Sammy was a healing balm for my family after the divorce.

When my dad met Sam for the first time, he pretended to love him, but I know now he was doing this for our sake. He even offered that Sammy could come stay at his house next time Jack and I came over, which made us so excited. Sammy became a constant for Jack and me. He would cuddle with us at Mom's and Dad's, and we would call dibs and end up fighting over who would get to sleep with Sammy for the night. If you're thinking to yourself that you're not a dog person, and this could never work for you, neither was my dad, but Sammy started growing on him. He even started to be sad when we didn't bring Sammy over.

With my dad's nice furniture and carpet, Sammy was a great dog because he was hypoallergenic, so he didn't shed. My dad, being selfless and wanting to make us feel better, put his preferences aside so that Jack and I could enjoy the constant of having Sammy. He showed us that he realized that the divorce affected us too.

Parents, stay with me here. I know it is hard when you yourself are just trying to survive. To consider adding one more creature under your feet to look after and care for can seem daunting. But your children will appreciate your selflessness when you allow this animal to come in and provide comfort when they too need it most.

LET'S GET PRACTICAL...

I know not all people are dog lovers and that's fine. The point of this tip was to express the huge help that Sammy was to our family. There are studies on how pets release calming and happy chemicals in our brains, which is why so many of us love them.

Your family constant might be a fish, a cat, or a guinea pig—start wherever is comfortable. You'll be surprised to see what comfort a pet can bring out in your child—they might start to gain greater responsibility for something larger than themselves and have a cuddle buddy when you're not in the mood. And maybe, just maybe, the pet might start to make its way into your heart as well.

ACTION PLAN

Analyze your current situation. What can you afford/what is allowed? Can you have a pet if you live in an apartment complex? If your kids want a dog, what kind would be best for your family's needs?

FOR YOUR CONSIDERATION/GOING DEEPER

1.) When growing up, did you have animals? If so, what kind of value did it add to your household?

_____

_____

_____

_____

_____

_____

_____

_____

_____

2.) How do you think an animal might help add stability and responsibility to your child's life?

_____

_____

_____

_____

_____

_____

_____

3.) If I didn't convince you to get an animal, then what other thing could be a constant source of comfort for your kid? Is it an object? A practice? A memory?

_____

_____

_____

_____

_____

_____

_____

_____

_____

_____

8

COMFORT IS A PHONE CALL AWAY

• • •

When I was younger, I would miss whichever parent I was not with for that weekend—it was a "grass is always greener on the other side" mindset. My parents caught onto this quickly because I would always ask to call or text the other parent. I wouldn't be away from the other parent for too long but, regardless, the pain of missing them felt *so* deep.

One thing that both of my parents did really well was letting me express my feelings. If I was missing my mom or dad, I wasn't told to suck it up or was met with defensive jealousy. Instead, they let me miss them. However, they didn't just leave me in that state of mind but let me call the other parent. My mom and I were super close when I was younger and being away from her was especially hard for me, so I would call her a lot.

Additionally, this was when my anxiety was bad, and I had separation anxiety with her. As time went on, and I became a teenager, I started to butt heads with my mom, calling my dad and meeting him at our local shopping mall on weeknights to get dinner more often.

I tell you this to reassure you that every child goes through stages. When your child is at a certain age and you see they are clinging to Dad more, that's okay—let them. If you try and pry them away and convince them that *you're* the fun and comforting parent, it might cause them to run even further.

There is no "winning" in this, it is not a competition. Mom doesn't have to be better than Dad, and Dad doesn't have to be better than Mom. It's not as if you are the only fun, creative, and huggable one, leaving less for the other parent to claim, as there can be shared qualities between you two. I know you may feel like you're the fun parent, but your co-parent can also be fun too, which doesn't take away from *your* ability to be fun. Again, there's no "first place" and "second place."

You need to do your very best to support your child's relationship with their other parent. This means, allowing them to talk to the other parent when they feel they need to.

LET'S GET PRACTICAL...

Maybe you're worried that your child is too young to have a cell phone, and that's fair. Luckily, they don't need one. Either your child can use your co-parent's phone to call you or, you can consider getting your child the Gabb Phone, a smartphone that can only call, text, play music, and take pictures—no internet, no social media. You don't have to worry about random, harmful ads and social media accounts. I am *not* sponsored by Gabb; I was just pleasantly surprised a product like this existed. In my mind, it's brilliant.

ACTION PLAN

Think through how to support your child having consistent contact with their other parent.

FOR YOUR CONSIDERATION/GOING DEEPER

1.) What are your current views on phone usage for your child? Do you think these ideas have changed post-divorce?

_____

_____

_____

_____

_____

_____

_____

_____

2.) What might be some potential challenges with your child having consistent contact with their other parent, and how might you deal with those constructively?

_____

_____

_____

_____

_____

_____

_____

_____

_____

_____

_____

_____

3.) What are some ways that you can reassure your child
that they have the freedom to call you and their other
parent when they want to?

_____

_____

_____

_____

_____

_____

_____

_____

_____

_____

_____

_____

9

TEACH YOUR KIDS TO FIND THE GOOD

• • •

I know, I know—you're probably wanting to skip this chapter just from reading the title. "Find the good"—is she serious? But that is exactly why I titled it this way; it says *find*. When I think of the word find, I see someone having to explore, to dig through dirt, to have hope for what they're about to encounter. To find the good does not mean to skip along and sing Kumbaya over the realities of divorce. But as the parent, you are someone your child looks to for affirmation, safety, and assurance; therefore, you need to have hope. Do you want your child to remember you as paralyzed by the divorce, always mad at their co-parent, and carrying bitterness? Or do you want your child to look back and remember that you went through one of the toughest things in your life and kept going?

If you are still reading, I am assuming you want to become the latter of the two, the one who kept going, so let's talk about the value of attitude. A positive mindset can really shape your attitudes and how you express them. Whether you tend to the positive or the negative, your emotions are contagious. Your kids are watching and will most likely take on whatever posture of heart you have.

For example, think of when you are with a friend at lunch and they recite a litany of complaints: their boss is a jerk, gas prices are through the roof, when is winter going to be finished, my taxes are due. On and on they drone and, before you know it, you too are jumping in with your very own complaints. I leave that type of situation feeling uneasy and unexcited about what's next. That is why your attitude and the words you speak matter, because your speech impacts yourself *and* your kids. Kids will follow your lead.

Your language around your kids is crucial, particularly the way you speak about your co-parent. I get that divorce may have not been in your plan, and that whatever went down between you and your co-parent hurt bad and might still hurt. I also understand the protective nature of parents. There may be times when you feel tempted to share with your child things about the other parent. You might even feel the urge to tell them your version of "the truth".

Can I be real with you?

You aren't protecting them in any way by doing that. Rather, you are changing their perception of their parent. They may be even looking for that instance that you warned them about to occur, living in fear rather than being present with their other parent.

Your child needs to figure out their opinions of their parent on their own—they don't need your help in this area. Yes, there is something to be said for telling your kids why you got a divorce, and that is a part of the healing process. However, you can read other books on how and when to do that part.

When *both* parents speak poorly about each other to their child, the child doesn't know who is right or wrong. Now the child can't trust either of their parents. So please,

I am begging you, don't speak poorly about your co-parent in front of your child. These feelings and thoughts need to be expressed, but save it for your therapist, sister, brother, or neighbor.

LET'S GET PRACTICAL...

I want to introduce you to a little thing called a life-giving list. You want to make these lists when you have space to brainstorm and use creative thinking. That way, when you are struggling and need to think of a positive activity to choose, the choices are right in front of you! No willpower or decision making necessary.

A life-giving list has three sections.

The first section includes things that are accessible, the second are those needing a little more planning, and the third are those requiring long term planning/big dreams. Within these sections you write what "gives you life." There is no formula to this, because what may give me life/joy may not give you life/joy.

For me, my accessible list has essential oils, playing the *Dirty Dancing* soundtrack in my car and yelling it, and taking a nap to rain sounds. For my second level, I have kayaking at the marina, seeing a movie with friends, and creating a craft from Pinterest. For my long-term list, I have visiting my friends in Missouri, holding a sloth, and becoming a public speaker.

Create these lists with your kids! There may be two, one for each house. After you create your lists, they are there to look at whenever you feel like divorce is trying to have the final word of your day. This list takes away the pressure of figuring out what to do when you're at a low point. You can pick something from the list to fit whatever energy level you're experiencing.

ACTION PLAN

Create your life-giving lists with your kids and pull it out when you are in need of a quick dose of joy! This should help everyone find and feel the good again
in some small ways.

FOR YOUR CONSIDERATION/GOING DEEPER

1.) Is your divorce the kind where it's easier to see the positives of the change? Or are these harder for you to see? What positives can you list for yourself or your kids?

_____

_____

_____

_____

_____

_____

_____

_____

_____

_____

2.) It's easy to be around others that will try and name your feelings for you. How will you stand firm in your waves of grief, positivity, freedom, and confusion? Who are safe people in your life that will let you fluctuate—not expecting you to be one thing?

_____

_____

_____

_____

_____

_____

_____

_____

_____

_____

3.) What habits or actions can you put in place to create better rhythms of positivity? Is it a yoga routine? A board with your favorite encouraging quotes? A collage of your favorite moments?

_____

_____

_____

_____

_____

_____

_____

_____

_____

_____

_____

Further Reading / Other Resources:

- *Atlas of the Heart* by Brené Brown — A book on language and words to use when we describe our feelings to one another and ourselves.

10

EMPOWER YOUR KIDS TO SPEAK UP

• • •

The main reason why I am writing this book is to speak on behalf of children who don't usually get the spotlight when one hears the word "divorce." I can *attempt* to speak for them through this book, but I can't touch everything, especially because every divorce is unique. I want to empower your child to learn to speak for themselves too.

That is why my next tip is to encourage your child to be courageous and speak up for themselves. I want your child to feel enabled to speak up if they feel something is wrong when they are at either parent's house.

Now, I bet some of you might be thinking, "Yeah, they need to speak up when something is off at my co-parent's house, but never at my own home!" I want to stop you there before moving on. This mindset is toxic for both you and your child. It's toxic for you to believe that you could never make a mistake—you're human. It also villainizes your co-parent which, remember, is still your child's other parent. Humble yourself and accept that you could still have blind spots and hurt your child's feelings without realizing it. Be careful about the ways in which you speak about their parent in front of them.

Speaking up for yourself is something that everyone has to learn how to do. This tip is not just for your kids, but also for you. I have seen relationships where one partner feels like they are powerless and could never speak up to the other, or that speaking up would only make things messier. In my own life, I have confronted people that I knew would never accept my point, but I had to do it out of having compassion for myself. It will be harder for your child to cultivate this in their lives if you don't live it out in your life.

What I want your child to know is that being courageous isn't getting rid of fear, it's doing something in spite of the fear present. Whether it has to do with divorce, school, or friends, help your child to learn how to speak up for themselves.

I know some kids whose mom or dad speak up for them to the other parent. When divorce came along, that kid no longer had their parent to lean on; they had to do it *themselves* instead. Growing up is hard enough as it is but having to grow up early because of the painful realities of divorce makes it even more challenging.

However, this pain can shape and mold your kid into a mature and compassionate person. I see that in my younger brother, Jack, who had to grow up fast and is now one of the most mature, kind-hearted young adults I have ever met. But growing up fast can also have the opposite effect, creating immature, bitter, and negative people. The outcome depends on a lot of factors, but one of the strongest is a presence or lack of a support system.

My parents let Jack and me speak our minds, be angry, and express our needs no matter how valid or invalid my parents may have thought our feelings were.

This brings me to my next point. You may not agree with your child's perspective; however, if your child is speaking up about it, it's a big deal, and it means that they trust you enough to express what they are feeling. If you don't agree with them or fully understand their perspective, ask clarifying questions instead of accusing ones. While a question can be both, your tone and phrasing determine its reception.

For example, instead of asking, "Why did you say that about me?" you can ask, "What am I doing to make you feel like I am mean?" Beyond asking clarifying questions, I would tell your kids directly that they have permission to come to you with anything, and that they can always speak up if they don't like something you're doing.

LET'S GET PRACTICAL...

Truthfully, the act of speaking up doesn't excite many people. I understand why this tip might feel scary, as you're entering unknown terrain, so I wanted to give you alternative ways to promote healthy means of speaking up within your household. Maybe you'll even learn to love these and take them to your workplace.

The first way you can help your child learn how to speak up is through providing a framework or an example. You can write, "I feel (insert emotion) because (insert reason or cause)" on a note card and tape it to their mirror or put it on the fridge. You can even print off a feelings wheel (which can be found on Google) to help them describe their feelings more in depth than simply sad, happy, or mad.

Another way to practice speaking up is to speak through writing. You can make an "I feel …" or "I want you to know" box for them to put pieces of paper with their feelings in it, and you can call the box whatever you want. You can invite your child to help you decorate the box, and through this activity, explain its purpose. You can read their slips at a time convenient to you—it can be on your own time or during a designated family dinner where you can read the slips together and talk about them.

I find the family dinner to be the best idea, if only because of the cushion and buffer of a meal for such a discussion.

Regardless, no matter how you choose to go about making space for your kids to truthfully share their feelings, make sure to thank your child for having the courage to speak up. They should be affirmed, not punished, when they speak honestly. If you are hurt, you too can be honest and tell them that what they had to say was hard for you to hear, but you are grateful that they called you out. Remember to apologize if feelings were hurt, and tell them that you will try your very best to not repeat that behavior. Remind your child that this is your first time parenting after divorce and you too are learning.

ACTION PLAN

Create that speak-up box and let it be a place for you and your kids to drop in notes of topics they want to address.

FOR YOUR CONSIDERATION/GOING DEEPER

1.) Is sharing how you feel scary for you? Why or why not?

_____

_____

_____

_____

_____

_____

_____

_____

_____

2.) How can you create safe spaces where your child feels the freedom to speak up about anything?

_____

_____

_____

_____

_____

_____

_____

_____

_____

3.) What phrases or encouraging words do you want to have in your back pocket for when your child speaks up?

_____

_____

_____

_____

_____

_____

_____

_____

11

DON'T SHOOT THE MESSENGER!

• • •

There is a spectrum of divorce ranging from low
conflict to high conflict. In low conflict, you see both
parents trying to put aside their opinions for the sake of
the child, keeping conflict to a minimum. In high conflict,
however, the relationship can sometimes include abuse
and dangerous situations for the kids.

No matter where you are on this spectrum, all parents
are susceptible to making the mistake of using their child
as a messenger.

Nobody likes being the messenger between two people. Being used as a messenger when you are a child of divorce is when the parent asks something like, "Hey, can you tell your dad if he is late again, I am not going to talk to him ever again?"

This is especially difficult for a kid who loves both of their parents. Having to tell Mom that she's late for her alimony payment—information a child only knows on behalf of their dad—is very uncomfortable.

Luckily, my parents were good at not doing this much. I can only recall a few times when this happened and it was simple stuff like, "Tell your mom her check is coming this weekend," or, "Tell your dad I sent him the basketball schedule over email." I say this because I have plenty of friends who've been messengers for awkward things—like financial matters or even dating.

You may be doing this to avoid conflict with your co-parent or avoid speaking to them, which I understand. However, when you are putting your child in charge of delivering a message to your co-parent, you are communicating to that child they hold all responsibility of maintaining harmony and communication between you and your co-parent.

Remember, your child is still a kid. Even if they display great communication skills and maturity, it's not their responsibility to be a messenger.

Let your kids be kids.

Let their only concern be if they got their homework done on time, not if they delivered the right message to their other parent.

LET'S GET PRACTICAL...

What should you do instead? Talk to your co-parent! I'm not saying you need to call them daily or even weekly and update them on everything. Instead, find a way that works for you depending on where you are on the conflict spectrum.

For your boundaries and safety, it may be that a journal goes back and forth between you and your co-parent, in which you both write to each other. It may be using texting or email only, or a quick 10-minute chat when you drop off the kids and update each other on logistics. It may be using an *adult* friend as a mediator if it's really bad.

All those options are great because they don't involve the child. Let the child focus on going back and forth from house to house, without the hassle of remembering what Dad needs to hear from Mom or vice versa.

ACTION PLAN
Get an envelope and put it somewhere you look often. This can serve as a visual reminder that your kids are not the messenger.

FOR YOUR CONSIDERATION/GOING DEEPER
1.) Have you ever felt stuck in the middle between two people you cared about? How did it make you feel?

_____

_____

_____

_____

_____

_____

_____

_____

_____

2.) Have there been times in the past when you have put your child in the role of messenger? What could you do differently moving forward to take your child out of that role?

_____

_____

_____

_____

_____

_____

_____

_____

3.) Brainstorm ways you could improve or change your ongoing communication with your co-parent so you don't put your child in the middle of the two of you.

_____

_____

_____

_____

_____

_____

_____

12

IT'S NOT BROKEN,
IT'S WHOLE

• • •

"Oh, I'm so sorry!"

"What was it like growing up in a broken home?"

"Wow, I bet the divorce was so hard. You probably wish your parents would get back together, right?"

I hear these reactions often when I tell people my parents divorced when I was eight. People have good intentions and yes, divorce is sad, but let me tell you, divorce didn't break my family, it made it more *whole*. My mom and dad are such different people now than when they were together—divorce allowed them the freedom to be their *whole* selves. Jack and I were also able to be with our mom and dad without walking on eggshells. The divorce gave us freedom; we were free from high-stress, honeycomb hideouts, and seeing only parts of parents' true selves.

Now, I get to see my mom in her fullness and my dad in his fullness—it's wonderful!

I hate book covers for divorce that show a physical home cracking in half or a child ripping up a piece of paper with a family drawn on it—these do not paint the full picture. I believe that when parents split, it doesn't mean that there are now two half units of what was once one family, but instead those two pieces are one full unit each, whole in and of themselves.

Sadly, there are so many stereotypes about divorce. It is not the end of a family, but rather the end of a marriage. The family continues but in a new way.

Additionally, it's not the worst thing to occur in one's life, because I have plenty of friends who wish their parents would have just divorced, since it was more harmful for everyone that they stayed together than if they had split.

It's always nice when I bring a friend to my mom's or my dad's house and they notice the health of my family dynamics. This doesn't mean we don't have our moments, and I am not saying divorce hasn't caused issues in my life —it has—but it's not the end of the story. It enabled my family to communicate better, be more themselves, and make choices for their best interest.

So no, my family is not broken—it is very much *whole*.

LET'S GET PRACTICAL...

Just like you may need reminders from friends that your story is not over, your kids will need reminders too. Remind them often that they are deeply loved by a whole family, and your family is not broken.

ACTION PLAN

Get a stone or something that reminds you of what it means to be whole. Keep it with you. In your pocket, your purse, your car dashboard. Hold it in moments when you need reminding that you and your kids *can* and *will* get through this tough time.

FOR YOUR CONSIDERATION/GOING DEEPER

1.) How can you reinforce a sense of family for your children and remind them that while the marriage may have ended, their family will continue?

_____

_____

_____

_____

_____

_____

_____

_____

_____

_____

2.) What are some of the stereotypes that you have heard when you tell others about your divorce? How does this make you feel?

_____

_____

_____

_____

_____

_____

_____

_____

_____

_____

_____

_____

_____

3.) In what ways has divorce freed you to be your whole self?

_____

_____

_____

_____

_____

_____

_____

_____

_____

_____

_____

13

GIVING KIDS TOO MUCH TO CARRY

• • •

I didn't discover the term "parentification" until I started my podcast. It was through interviewing children of divorce and hearing their stories that I found that this term was very common. So many kids of divorce feel like they need to take care of their parent's emotional wellbeing. In venting to your child about your anger with your co-parent, your sadness about the split, or asking them advice—they feel needed in a way that isn't positive.

This relational dynamic creates *enmeshment* (a relationship between two or more people in which personal boundaries are permeable and unclear) and makes the child feel as though it is their job to keep Mom and Dad happy.

The term parentification comes from the idea that the child becomes the parent to their own parent. This isn't a divorce thing, as it can happen to any child, but it's more common in divorce stories. If you want to avoid creating this parental anxiety in your child, I have a few suggestions.

First, don't confide in your kids about adult matters, like your dating drama, anger with your co-parent, or wrestling with the past before your divorce. Asking for advice is tricky too. If you ask your child how to parent or discipline their younger sibling, that's parentifying. If you ask your child about how to talk to their other parent, that's parentifying. If you ask your child for hug when you're sad, that's—I'm just kidding, that's not parentifying, that's just letting yourself be human in front of your kids.

Of course, your child needs to see you sad, but what they also need is for you to tell them that sometimes you get sad, and that's normal, but that you would love a hug from them. All the while, remind your child that it is never their responsibility to make you happy.

One of my favorite episodes on my podcast is with my friend, Katherine. In this conversation we talk about how enmeshed Katherine and her mom were. She took pride in being able to read her mom like a book, always knowing exactly how to keep her happy. It wasn't until later in life that Katherine realized this was neither normal nor her responsibility.

If you've slipped up, it's not too late to make a change.

Know that mess ups are inevitable because you're human.

Give yourself some grace.

LET'S GET PRACTICAL...

Remember that your child is a child. Even if they are incredibly mature for their age, they are still a child, and their minds might not be able to handle the information you want to confide in them.

Instead, talk to your siblings, a counselor, a friend, a neighbor—anyone but your kid!

But be careful where you speak, because kids are sneaky and can overhear phone calls too. Go on a walk or a drive for your phone call and try your very best not to have conversations about your divorce or the other parent when your children are around.

ACTION PLAN

Have a list of people ready to call when you need to vent, cry, and talk about parenting. Pin this list up where you will see it to remember to stop before you unload on your kid.

FOR YOUR CONSIDERATION/GOING DEEPER

1.) After reading this, what are some ways you or your co-parent may have parentified your child?

_____

_____

_____

_____

_____

_____

_____

_____

_____

2.) What phrases will you use to remind your kids that they aren't responsible for your feelings?

_____

_____

_____

_____

_____

_____

_____

_____

_____

3.) Who can you turn to for support when things feel overwhelming or stressful?

_____

_____

_____

_____

_____

_____

_____

_____

_____

14

KIDS STILL NEED TO BE PARENTED

• • •

Children of divorce are not going to like me for this, but I have to confess … I have played the Divorce Card.

As embarrassing as this confession is, it's true. What is the Divorce Card, you may ask? If I really wanted something from one of my parents and they weren't going to give in, I would tell them that I was sad about the divorce or something related to the divorce. I know, I know, not a good look. But I say this to warn parents that it does happen. I think I picked this trick up when I was around 11-years-old, which is young!

As an elementary school teacher, I see kids playing similar cards all the time to get what they want. It's not just a thing for kids of divorce, as any smart child can see the way that people respond to certain tactics and use it to manipulate.

I want to challenge you to watch for this trick. Your kids are smart and preceptive, and they may notice that when they are having a hard "divorce day" you give them extra ice cream or let them have more iPad time. Those hard "divorce days" are real, and those feelings are valid!

However, don't let those become a pattern to where your child can put on a show to make you do whatever they desire. As Christina McGhee, co-parenting coach and guest on my podcast, put it: "The things that kids needed before the divorce—(love, discipline, shelter, food, routine) —kids will still need *after* the divorce."

Don't let the divorce create a lack of discipline or routines in your parenting. Of course, there are times to be extra gracious with them, create fun for them, and give them a break. I just don't want you to be stomped on by a smart kid who knows they can manipulate you to get what they want.

Once my parents started to catch onto my tricks—which usually showed up in the middle of the Target toy aisle—my parents started to put their foot down. What their "no" did for me was remind me I wasn't the authority and, in a strange way, this realization gave me comfort.

It's good to know that my parents could give me boundaries in my life, especially as a little one who doesn't have a fully-developed brain yet. Rules, structure, and boundaries are acts of love, I promise. In the moment, your child might despise them, but over time they will learn to love these limits, because they know what's expected of them. When you know what's expected of you, you know how to succeed.

It's why we have this thing at my elementary school called CHAMPS: **C**onversation level, how to ask for **H**elp, **A**ctivity, **M**ovement, **P**articipation, and if you follow these it leads to **S**uccess. These five expectations tell the kids what they need to do to be successful in class. To give you some background, my students have some pretty tough home lives that usually create unstable environments for them, which means that when they come back from a long weekend or a break, they are disoriented and hyper. They completely lose their routine at home, and they hate the

CHAMPS. However, after a few weeks they start to love the CHAMPS again—in fact, if I forgot to tell them what the conversation level is they will call me out and ask for it.

I tell you this example to show you that *all* kids need rules and expectations. Including kids of divorce.

LET'S GET PRACTICAL...

The ultimate dream would be for both co-parents to be on the same page for house rules and behavior expectations. However, this is not the case for many co-parents. My advice to you is to create structure, routine, and rules that *your* house abides by.

You can't control what your co-parent does, but you can make collaborative suggestions. Some of these things might already be in place, so this may not even call for a huge change. All I am saying is don't let your kids get whatever they want, eat all the sugar they want, or go out and party in high school every time they want because you and your co-parent got a divorce. Nice try, kids.

ACTION PLAN

Write out the basic ground rules for your house. Does anything need to change post-divorce? Do any new things need to be added? Do any things need to be removed?

FOR YOUR CONSIDERATION/GOING DEEPER

1.) When you were in school, how did you know what was expected of you in order to succeed? How might this same structure be applied to your home?

_____

_____

_____

_____

_____

_____

_____

_____

2.) Have there been times when you have given in with your kids because you felt guilty about the divorce and how it has changed their lives? What could you do moving forward to balance love and limits?

_____

_____

_____

_____

_____

_____

_____

_____

_____

_____

_____

_____

_____

3.) Is there a mantra or mission statement you want your house to be marked by? What do you want your home to feel like?

_____

_____

_____

_____

_____

_____

_____

_____

_____

_____

_____

15

CONSIDER YOUR KIDS WHEN DATING

• • •

About two years after the divorce, I remember my mom telling me about the first guy she liked, and I immediately got mad. I started crying, upset that she would bring a random guy into our little life of the three of us (her, my brother, and myself).

Keep in mind, she never introduced us, just simply brought him up.

Looking back now, I know my reaction was irrational and unfair to my mom. However, at the time, I was her protector. I didn't trust *anyone* to take care of her like Jack and I could. I know this hurt my mom, but she didn't show it. The reason I know it hurt her is because we share a nail technician, named Bea, who we've both been seeing since I was in second grade. If you know anything about getting any kind of beautification done, you know there is going to be gossip taking place.

As I got older and started to see Bea on my own, she told me how much my mom gave up for Jack and me. When I told her I was aware of this, she proceeded to tell me something I never knew, which is that my response to my mom dating made her commit to not dating until we were out of the house. I had no idea, and I felt so incredibly guilty. Bea told me not to tell my mom anything, but to proceed as if nothing happened.

The first time I met my dad's first girlfriend, I was in elementary school. I still remember her so vividly; she was funny, charismatic, and named after a superhero. We got to play games at Dave & Busters with her which, at that time, was all I needed to approve of her. For some reason, I didn't have the same intense emotional reaction as I did with my mom's love life.

Since then, my dad has dated others and I have always met them. However, he always made sure it was something serious before introducing us. Currently, neither of my parents are remarried. I know I am a rare child of divorce because I don't have any step—or, as I like to say, *bonus*—parents. But this is my story.

I tell you these two stories to paint a picture of two different paths you can go down. They are both the right choice. Why? Because they were chosen after careful consideration from my parents. They looked at their needs and desires and chose based on that.

For my mom, she wanted to preserve the chemistry that the three of us had and didn't want any other person adding to or taking away from that. She chose to use our childhood as a time to heal, discover new passions, and step up in using her voice.

My dad chose the right path for him because he needed a companion. He didn't get to see Jack and I as often and I know he got lonely—anyone would! Both of their choices were right for them, and right for Jack and me. That's what matters.

You get to do the same by looking at your circumstances, needs, and desires and then choosing what works for you and your family. It may take you a while to heal after the divorce before you can even begin thinking about getting yourself back out there.

For others, dating may come quickly. Let's face it, you're still human, and we all desire connection.

LET'S GET PRACTICAL...

As a child who has never been married or divorced, you can take this advice with as much weight as you would like. You have every right to write me off. However, this is a book by a child of divorce. So here is my perspective: don't introduce us to the new partner until you feel it has long term potential. This can help shield us from forming attachments to partners that may not be long term.

As a child of divorce, I can say it is very tough to hear that your parent and their girlfriend/boyfriend broke up, and often feels like another mini-divorce. It's hard to not get attached to them, wanting to bond with them and their kids as well. Therefore, if you can, try and introduce them to as few partners as possible. I can imagine it would be hard not to do this because your kids are such a big part of your world, but trust me, you are helping your kids by waiting.

Another thing that gets tangled in this are your new partner's kids (if they have any). When your kids meet their kids, hopefully they get along and befriend one another.

I know someone whose dad dated a woman for six years and she had kids—they all became friends with one another over time. Unfortunately, the relationship didn't last, and the dad told the kids that they had to unfollow the girlfriend's kids on all their social media and cut off all contact. This was really hard for the kids—not only were they sad about losing that girlfriend in their life, but now they had to say goodbye to friends. My friend would've preferred the dad to let the kids stay friends.

Blending a possible family is hard, and each family is different; just don't forget that kids mourn breakups too.

ACTION PLAN

If you decide to start dating, let your kids know that you are spending time with other adults. You can also share that for now you are choosing not to introduce them to people you are dating however, when someone becomes important to you they will be the first to know. Remind them that they are always going to be your loves!

FOR YOUR CONSIDERATION/GOING DEEPER

1.) Who is going to help you decide your path to dating? Let it be someone who knows you and your experiences well.

_____

_____

_____

_____

_____

_____

_____

_____

2.) Imagine from the perspective of your children, how it feels to see a parent with someone new. What are some feelings or worries you think your kids might have? What could you do to reassure them? Try to picture it from the perspective of your children, especially if they are different ages—this feels different at eight than it does at seventeen.

_____

_____

_____

_____

_____

_____

_____

_____

_____

_____

_____

3.) How will you know when you are ready to start dating again? How will you know when you are ready to introduce your kids to someone new? How will you know when they are ready to meet someone new?

_____

_____

_____

_____

_____

_____

_____

_____

_____

_____

_____

16

WRITE YOUR OWN TIPS

• • •

Just like that, I am now handing the torch to you. This is probably my favorite tip because this will apply most easily to your specific situation. Why? Because the tips come from you and your child, and no one knows your situation better. You can now write your own tips to aid you through your divorce. I would start by writing down tips that will help you stay accountable as a parent after reading this book.

Next, you can make another set of tips as a family with your kids. As I have said throughout, it's all about how you frame the activity, so make it fun. Devote a night to hosting a big brainstorming session to create your own tips. You can make your own pizzas that night, wear goofy costumes, or build a fort to house the brainstorming party.

If your child is older, then make the party more accommodated to what they like—this might involve s'mores around the fire as your child talks about what things they want to remind themselves of while healing and coping with divorce. (So many of my tips revolve around food, but that is because food is where all my major conversations with people have occurred—it has a way of opening people up).

A crucial part of these brainstorming parties needs to be the freedom to say anything, as we have discussed previously. There is no such thing as a bad idea or an idea that is too small—look at my tips, where I wrote one just about a dog. It might seem small, but it had incredible impact. Additionally, it's small, intentional actions that create a healthy and safe environment for your child to call home. Another thing to remember is that this event does not need to be a one-time occurrence—this list of tips can be added to overtime. There is no limit on the number of tips.

I would say the more tips, the better… I know as a child of divorce, I needed all the help I could get!

LET'S GET PRACTICAL…

Brainstorming might give you a case of writer's block. To combat this, you need some tools. My favorites are a giant white board with markers, crayons, paper, sticky notes, and of course, a laser pointer (if you're extra like I am). Laser pointer or not, think about what might work best for you and your kids and what you'll need to get the ball rolling.

ACTION PLAN

Plan your brainstorming event with your kids and write your own tips as a family! Bonus: let your co-parent know you're doing this and see if they would do it for their house!

FOR YOUR CONSIDERATION/GOING DEEPER

1.) What are the main things you took away from this book?

_____

_____

_____

_____

_____

_____

_____

_____

_____

_____

_____

_____

2.) How did this book relate to your circumstances? How are yours different?

_____

_____

_____

_____

_____

_____

_____

_____

_____

_____

_____

3.) What do you want your kids to remember their parents were like when they grow up?

_____

_____

_____

_____

_____

_____

_____

_____

_____

_____

_____

_____

_____

EPILOGUE
Thank you for your humility.

You did it! I would like to take a moment to thank you. **Thank you for humbling yourself by taking advice from someone who is probably younger than you, and someone who has never been a parent and hasn't been through a divorce herself.** I hope you learned something from these chapters and feel more connected to your child's perspective.

I hope these chapter titles are on your fridge, in your backpacks, on car dashboards, or on your newest phone background. I hope these ideas are not just talked about for a day or two, but rather something that can guide you through this season continuously. Don't be afraid to include your kids in the conversations; consider doing a weekly check-in to see if you all are living by your own tips or if some tips need to be added to your toolbox.

Just by reading this book you are already one step ahead in fighting for your child's healing. The goal isn't to make this a painless process for them, but to make it one that they look back on and see that you were with them, in the trenches, creating moments of hope and love during this uneasy time.

If this book helped you in anyway I'd love to hear about it! You can leave a review on Goodreads, Amazon, or email me at: grace@divorcetipsfromkids.com

Thank you for your time.

APPENDIX

5th Grade Grace's Original Tips to Kids

Tip #1:
Experiment with the Schedule To Find One That Works!

I need two weekends in a row with my mom to feel ready to spend one weekend with my dad. So that's one tip if you don't know how to schedule everything you can try that. See if you like it, because it works for me!

Tip #2:
Plan Your Own Fun!

When I go to my dad's house, my brother and I bring over our own backpacks. The backpacks can be filled with fun family things such as: coloring books, play dough, legos, movies, and favorite snacks.

P.S.) If your mom and dad always have stuff planned you can still bring the backpacks because you will be prepared if plans fall through.

Tip #3:
Get Rid of Worries

If you ever worry about anything... because face it, there are lots of worries in divorce: Do we have enough money? Is dad ok? Is mom happy?

...keep a journal handy; journaling is actually healthy for your body, heart, and mind. It's good to get things out.

Tip #4:
Take Mom and Dad with You Wherever You Go

When I'm at my dad's I bring a T-shirt of my mom's that's sprayed with her perfume that I sleep with. You see, my mom wears perfumes and lotions that make her smell like her. I'm not saying she stinks, I'm saying she smells like my mom and that smell reminds me of how much we love each other.

Tip #5:
Don't Doubt the Love

Just to let you know, even though your parents are divorced or separated, no matter what I bet you $20 bucks that they will always love you (and that's a lot of money)!

Tip #6:
Squeeze Your Stress Away

If you have a lot of stress when you go to one of your parent's houses, you can make a stress ball. Just get a balloon, put a funnel in the hole, and pour flour in it. So now when you're stressed out you can squeeze it or use Tip #3.

Tip #7:
The Power of Pets

If you have a pet, ask if you can take it to either your mom or dad's house; or ask if you can have a pet, so that it will be waiting to welcome you when you come to stay.

Tip #8:
Comfort is a Phone Call Away

Whenever you start to miss your mom or dad, just call them; it will make you feel a lot better. For example, my mom just bought me a cell phone that I can only use when I want to call my dad or my mom. Not friends! It makes me feel real comfortable.

Tip #9:
Stay Positive

I think a positive attitude is the real key to each house. I have found out that when I have a positive attitude no matter what, nothing seems to go so wrong that it defeats me. Some ways to get a positive attitude:

1. Remember "this won't last forever" if you are in a difficult time
2. Listen to your favorite music
3. Do something for someone else, like make a card for dad when you are at your mom's.

Tip #10:
Be Courageous... Speak Up

Always try and speak up for yourself (or maybe even your younger siblings).

ACKNOWLEDGEMENTS

This short, easy read may look simple, but so much time and care was put into it. I need to thank many of the individuals who cheered on this project one way or another.

Thank you to the woman who first named this a book when I was ten, Sharon Hersh. Thank you to my coach in the publishing world, Don Pape. Thank you to the man who gifted me his e-course and filled me with such wonder, Taylor Hughes. Thank you to HD Tolson who polished my writing and made sure I communicated my ideas with excellence. Thank you to Christina McGhee who believed in this project enough to give me critical feedback. You're a pioneer in the divorce and children space, and I wouldn't have the opportunities I have now without your work. Thank you for the time that you put into this project.

I couldn't have kept up the vision, drive, or execution of this book without my loving friends and family. Thank you to my mom and dad. Without you two, this project wouldn't even exist. Thank you for choosing what was right for each other and what was right for Jack and I. Thank you to my siblings: Jessica, Jeff, Jack, and yes even my sibling through marriage, Andy. Thank you to my high school and college friends—you stayed up with me during late nights, funded my coffee shop visits, and always asked me, "How is the book going?"

Thank you to all the divorced moms and dads who have supported me via social media and listened to my podcast. Those who have subscribed, left a review, and continued to remind me of my why.

Kids of divorce—thank you. You are the reason why I wrote this book. You continue to inspire me and remind me why this work is so important. I want to challenge you to use your divorce story to help other kids of divorce. Together, we can create a larger space for kids of divorce to share their experiences, encourage one another, and be there for each other in the hard moments. You have endured something that you never asked for, and here you are, doing it. Finding the good, and reminding others that we are not from broken homes, but *whole* ones.

Made in the USA
Columbia, SC
26 May 2025

58457464R00079